**TRADITIONAL FALSEHOODS AND CREATIVE WHOPPERS
YOUR PARENTS TOLD YOU ABOUT SEX, LIFE, AND
SANTA CLAUS**

**DID YOU BELIEVE . . .**

*The stork brought you?*

*Play with it and it will fall off?*

*A summer in New Jersey will be just as fun as a summer in Europe?*

*I am listening?*

*No one will ever love you if: you bite your nails/pick your nose/don't clean your room?*

*Your belly button is where the angels poked you to see if you were done?*

**OF COURSE YOU DID.**

**AND MAYBE YOU STILL DO.**

*LIES MY PARENTS TOLD ME*

*St. Martin's Paperbacks Titles
by Bernice Kanner*

ARE YOU NORMAL?
LIES MY PARENTS TOLD ME

# LIES MY PARENTS TOLD ME

### BERNICE KANNER

St. Martin's Paperbacks

LIES MY PARENTS TOLD ME

Copyright © 1996 by Bernice Kanner.

ISBN: 0-312-95999-0

Printed in the United States of America

St. Martin's Paperbacks trade paperback edition/June 1996

10  9  8  7  6  5  4  3  2  1

# TABLE OF CONTENTS

# LIES MY PARENTS TOLD ME

# INTRODUCTION

Webster's 20th Century defines lies as "false statements made with the intent to deceive." In many cases, lies our parents told us were meant to deceive; just as often they were noble artful deceptions meant to build confidence or character or to keep us from harm or preserve the sanctity of childhood.

While 91 percent of Americans say they lie regularly, not all those lies are knowing. Sometimes, parents lie unintentionally. "You're beautiful," muttered to a gawky ten-year-old with glasses and braces isn't necessarily a fib. A mom sees beyond the ugly duckling to the person she's birthed: blood of her blood, loin of her loins, and often, enactment of her dreams. To her, that ugly duckling might truly be a swan. And surely, "No one will notice" can be construed as more kind than cruel.

Similarly, some lies are simply misconceptions about life that the parent herself believes—or can't bear not to:

"Killing is okay if you do it for your country."

"The law and government are here to help you."

"Jewish men put you on a pedestal."

"Big boys don't cry."

"Women over 40 don't have long hair."

"The Yankees are always in the World Series.

"We are the chosen people."

"He died peacefully."

**And what of Santa Claus and the Tooth Fairy? These are gifts, these lies, we give our children, to preserve their innocence and sense of wonder. These lies are different from the kinds husbands and wives tell each other.**

**Some lies, of course, are cut from the same cloth: mom or dad is caught in the act and has to do some fancy maneuvering to extricate him or herself.**

"I wasn't reading your diary. I was looking for my contact lens."

"I wasn't waiting up. I was watching a movie."

"I wasn't listening in on your phone call; I was trying to call Aunt Mary."

"We're related. This is Uncle Bill."

**So many lies our parents have told us are "old wives' tales," healthful remedies that sometimes, it's discovered, contain more than a germ of truth.**

"Coffee stunts your growth."

"An apple a day keeps the doctor away."

"Aspirin with Coca-Cola will make you high and crazy."

"Eat raw potatoes and you'll get worms."

"Soak your feet in hot mustard oil and your earache will disappear."

"Red pepper keeps the devil away." (So do four-leaf clover, saints medals, and mandrake root).

**Others are sheepdogs or dray horses, harnessed with heavy loads of consequence, to keep children in line. Some are designed to keep us from doing something—to manipulate our behavior.**

"If you don't behave, the pilot will turn the plane around right now."

"You get sties in your eyes from peeing in the road."

"If you don't wash behind your ears potatoes will grow there."

"Twenty-five cents a week is what every 14-year-old gets for an allowance."

"Sex isn't fun until you're married."

"Going out with a wet head will give you pneumonia."

"*Everyone*'s wearing navy."

"You can get pregnant from sitting on a public toilet."

"What vegetables? That's a salami soufflé."

"Boys just want one thing."

"Loafers make your feet spread."

"Masturbation makes you go blind."

"Cross your eyes and they'll stick that way for life."

"Don't show your boyfriend your report card; it will make him feel inadequate."

"Keep playing with it and it will fall off."

"Polish the apple before eating it or you'll rouse the devil's ire."

"Your nose grows when you tell a lie."

**Others are more proactive:**

"Carrots will make you see in pitch darkness."

"Hand-me-downs are fun."

**Still others take a stab at explaining the world, sometimes truthfully, but more often idealistically. Some are lies we believe way into adulthood.**

"Get a teaching degree so you'll have something to fall back on."

"Everything works out for the best."

"The stork brought you."

"We're not getting a dog because your mother is allergic to animal hair."

"Geometry comes in handy later in life."

"You have to suffer to be beautiful." (*Il faut suffrir d'etre belle.*)

"Freckles are God's kisses."

"Those [sanitary napkins] are a new kind of dinner napkin."

## Others seem to be simply drawn from thin air.

"A dog's breath will melt your bones."

"Your belly button's where the angels poked you to see if you were done."

"Don't sleep with a pumpkin in the room; it will suck the air out and you'll die."

## Still others try to keep the peace.

"Your brother wasn't trying to kill you when he pushed you off the top of the slide."

"Just ignore the bully and he'll stop."

"Your sister isn't hitting you. Those are love taps."

## Some put a bright light on things:

"Pulling out weeds is good exercise."

"It's never too late."

## Others are promises broken or demoralizing dark notes:

"We'll go camping together next summer, just the two of us."

"I'll be back in five minutes."

"My, isn't that hairdo attractive?"

"No one will ever love you."

**And of course, there are the "be-grateful, we-had-it-so-hard" series that invariably begin "When I was your age..."**

"When I was your age I walked eight miles to school—and back again." (Often this hike was done in deep snow, without shoes or warm coat, no doubt carrying heavy bundles on an empty stomach. In many households, the trip was uphill both ways.)

**In a similar vein:**

"This hurts me more than it hurts you."

"I'm doing this for your own good."

**And, of course:**

"Someday you'll thank me for this."

**My parents are no longer among the living: I cannot laugh or scowl at their lies any longer—or even hold them for accounting. I can only remember them fondly—or otherwise—and catch myself repeating fibs they told me to my own children.**

**I have asked Americans of all ages the lies they remember their parents telling them.**

# ONCE UPON A TIME ... THE CLASSICS

People have defined the three stages of a person's life as believing in Santa Claus, not believing in Santa Claus, and being Santa Claus. Lies our parents tell occur most often when we're in stage one—the age of innocence—and they're in stage three.

- Be good or Santa Claus won't bring you any toys.

- Once upon a time . . .

- A pot of gold can be found at the end of the rainbow.

- Leprechauns (trolls, fairies, fairy godmothers, gnomes, elves) live here.

- Fairies are real. When you say you don't believe in them, one dies a wee bit.

- She is a fairy princess.

- A dwarf's gift is a pot of gold.

- The Easter Bunny will hide the eggs, but give you candy in return.

- The Tooth Fairy knows the going rate.

- Don't worry about the monsters under your bed. Dad has his .44 loaded and will blow them away if they so much as try anything.

- There is an Easter Bunny.

- There's a man in the moon.

- When you wish upon a star your dreams come true.

- Someday your prince will come.

- And they lived happily ever after.

- Santa and the reindeer enjoyed the snacks.

- Yes, Virginia, there is a Santa Claus.

# I Wasn't . . .

**It's not just kids who get caught in the act—or who invent some excuse for what they've done—or failed to do. Parents caught with their hands in the cookie jar have come up with some imaginative explanations.**

- I wasn't listening in on your phone call; I was trying to call Aunt Mary.

- I wasn't littering; I was leaving food for the birds.

- I wasn't looking through your drawers; I was putting away the laundry.

- I was just trying to stop a nose bleed.

- I wasn't waiting up. I was watching a movie.

- I wasn't reading your diary; I was looking for my contact lens.

- I wasn't spying on you; your diary turned up on my bookshelf.

- It tastes better from the carton.

- We just remember it differently.

- I wasn't looking for dope in your pocketbook; I just wanted an aspirin.

- I wasn't looking for your diaphragm; I needed some tissues.

- I wasn't sleeping; I was reading.

- I didn't forget your birthday. I was planning a surprise later.

- As it so happens, I was talking to a lady from the church.

- I didn't dodge the draft. We were getting married anyway.

- I *am* listening.

- I have no idea what happened to your first-grade artwork.

- I was never too shy to call a girl.

- I *am* awake.

- I voted when you were at school.

- The devil made me do it.

- I had a flat tire.

- They're my friend's cigarettes.

- I had to work late.

- Daddy and I were just wrestling in bed when you walked in.

- Oh him? He's just a guy who came to read the meter.

- I wasn't eating your candy; I was checking to make sure it wasn't spoiled.

- She's just a friend.

- I wasn't dating her when I was married to your mother.

# On Lying

**"Your nose is growing" is but one of many misrepresentations parents have laid on us to keep us honest. . . .**

- Your nose grows when you tell a lie.

- I wouldn't lie to you.

- A light on your forehead glows when you tell a lie.

- You get pimples on your tongue when you tell a lie.

- It happened to Pinocchio, and it's happening to you.

- Your tongue goes black when you lie.

- I can always tell when you tell a lie.

- You start to sweat when you tell a lie.

- God knows when you're lying.

- God gave you hiccups for telling a lie.

**Not all lies are bad.**

• A little truth helps the lie go down.

• A little white lie won't hurt anybody.

• I was crossing my fingers; the lie didn't count.

• I don't want any yes boys around me. I want everybody to tell me the truth (even if they get punished for it).

• Tell white lies and you'll go color blind.

• When in doubt, tell the truth.

• Parents *never* lie to their children.

# When You're the Mother/Father

**Who could wait until the magic moment of adulthood when privileges and liberties would be conferred?**

- When you're the mother, you can do it your way.

- When you're the grown-up you can sit in the front seat.

- When it's your house you can keep it as filthy as you want.

- When you're the driver you can travel at any speed you want.

- When you're an adult your opinion will count.

- Because I'm the mother, that's why.

# IF YOU DON'T BEHAVE

**Sometimes parents resorted to creative rebukes to bring their offspring in line—to get them to settle down or shape up. More often than not, the punishments mom or dad dreamed up were idle threats, never to be doled out.**

- If you don't behave, the pilot will turn the plane around right now.

- St. Nick will know.

- Your father will deal with this.

- You won't go to camp this summer.

- You're grounded for life.

- No more TV for a week.

- I'm cancelling our Christmas trip.

- You'll send me to an early grave.

- We'll remember this when it comes time to buy birthday gifts.

- I'll throw out all your toys.

- Forget about your birthday party.

- If you don't stop fighting, I will shoot you both.

- Daddy and I will get a divorce because of this.

- That's it. I'm pulling over, and you're getting out and walking.

- I'll chop your head off.

- I'll pull your neck like a chicken.

- I'll hit you so hard your shirt will ride up your back like a window shade.

- If you don't eat your string beans you won't be able to see Bill. (But I saw him and he wasn't invisible.)

- That's enough.

- We'll find a new family for you.

- We'll take you to the orphanage.

- You're worse than Dennis the Menace.

- Your kids will do to you what you're doing to me.

- I'm going to talk to your teacher.

- When you have kids you grow extra eyes; your hair hides them.

- There's a spanking machine in the attic if you don't behave.

- I'm giving you one last chance.

# YOUR BROTHER/SISTER'S HERE

**Sibling rivalry posed big problems for parents who often resorted to inventive explanations and propaganda to greet his or her arrival—or rationalize hostile behavior.**

- We love you both the same.

- We loved you so much we wanted another just like you.

- All of you were planned.

- Your brother loves you.

- He's not a rival; he's a playmate.

- Your brothers and sisters are your best friends.

- Your sister isn't jealous of you; she wants you to do well.

- Your sister asked for you when she called.

- Blood is thicker than water.

- Your brother wasn't trying to kill you when he pushed you off the top of the slide.

# HAND-ME-DOWNS

**They didn't have to be hand-me-downs. They could be clothes on sale or a gift someone gave you that you wouldn't wear even to the bathroom, or just something your parents loved and wanted you to love too. In any case, the pressure was on to convince you that this was the item you'd been waiting for to complete your portfolio.**

• Hand-me-downs are fun.

• You'll grow into them.

• It's the latest thing.

• Everyone will be wearing a hat.

• Pink really is your color.

• It's an honor to wear your sister's clothes.

- That looks better on you than it did on your brother.

- He had it before it came into style. You're wearing it at its prime.

# Body parts

**Sure noses are for breathing and smelling and ears are for hearing, but to hear our parents tell it, there's often magic in their contours. And what about dimples and bellybuttons?**

- Your bellybutton is where the angels poked you to see if you were done.

- An "innie" means you're sweet and smart; an "outie" means you're creative and outgoing.

- Dimples are from sleeping on a stick.

- Very bright people have big ear lobes.

- Your eyes are the windows of your soul.

- Your freckles are God's kisses.

- You have two left feet.

- Going barefoot makes your feet big.

- Loafers spread your feet.

- If you eat your vegetables you'll have curly hair.

- This *is* my natural color.

- Short people have more fun.

- Good things come in small packages.

- Boys like short girls.

- Those aren't moles; they're beauty marks.

- You have birthmarks because someone threw black pepper on me when I was pregnant.

- Only tramps wear nail polish.

- You can tell a person's character if he bites his nails.

- The total number of white specks on your finger indicates the number of lies you've told.

- The tip of your nose is especially tasty.

# BULLIES

How did you deal with a class bully who made your life miserable? Parents operated under the delusion that calling the baddie on it would raise his consciousness—and curtail his behavior. Their suggestions:

• Just ignore him and he'll stop.

• Pity him; he's just insecure and can only lash out.

• You can't be mean and happy at the same time.

• He's just a small boy in a big body.

• He's just doing it to get a rise out of you.

• Sticks and stones will break your bones but names will never harm you.

• People listen to people who talk with their mouth, not their fists.

• The teacher will help solve it for you.

• I'm sure he's not trying to taunt you.

• A month from now you'll be good friends.

# BIRDS AND BEES

**Explaining the facts of life prompted so many euphemisms that many parents even referred to it as the birds and the bees. But getting teens to abstain from it often required a mix of pleading, deception, and propaganda. Much of this fibbing was to sheepdog us, to get us to suppress our urge and curiosity with threats of dire consequences.**

• All you have is your reputation.

• Good girls wait.

• You can tell me if you've had sex. I won't get mad.

• The two dogs stuck together out there sat in glue.

• Those are Egyptian balloons and I date the box to see how long they last, so stay out of them!

• No one will respect you if you're not a virgin.

• Virginity is good.

- Masturbation is evil.

- Masturbation leads to blindness.

- Masturbate and you'll have hair growing from the center of your palm.

- People who have sex before they're 18 are tramps.

- Sex isn't fun until you're married.

- Masturbation makes you sterile.

- Boys only want one thing.

- This sapphire ring should help keep your virginity.

- He'll tell you he's only putting it part of the way in.

- Men don't marry girls like that.

- Chastity belts are good.

- Men love it when you play hard to get.

- Those [condoms] are comb cleaners.

- If you touch your privates, your hand will turn black.

- Girls will lead you astray.

- He doesn't want you for yourself.

- You can wait about sex. It's not such a big deal.

- He won't buy the cow if he can have the milk for free.

- Play with it and it will fall off.

# GETTING PREGNANT

**Getting pregnant was the great no-no of all time, the event that would ruin our lives and destroy our family. But to hear our parents tell it, it could happen in ways other than biological union.**

- If you sit in his lap, you'll get pregnant.

- If you kiss him, you'll get pregnant.

- If you go to the drive-in, you'll end up pregnant.

- You'll get pregnant if you swallow a pumpkin seed.

- If you sit on a public toilet seat, you'll get pregnant.

- She got pregnant because she used the same bath water as her brother.

- You wear clothes like that and you'll wind up pregnant.

- No one in our family has ever had a child out of wedlock.

- Abortion is for other people.

- If you get her pregnant, the judge will throw you in prison.

- It will kill your father.

# BEWARE

**Parents often try to create some terror in a child to make sure he or she stays away from dangers that can be avoided. Often this results in dire predictions of gloom.**

## KEEP AWAY

- The dog in that yard attacks stragglers.

- It has medicine in it.

- That house is haunted.

- There are big rodents and gators in the river.

- The fence is wired to electrocute.

- Eat in the bathroom and the devil will get you.

## YOU'LL GO BLIND (AND OTHER EYE PROBLEMS)

- You'll go blind if you watch TV in the dark.

- You can go blind if you look into the eyes of your mother-in-law.

- You'll go blind reading under the covers.

- You'll go blind reading in a dark room.

- Cross your eyes and they'll stick that way for life.

- You get sties in your eyes from peeing in the road.

- If someone presses on your neck, your eyeballs will pop out.

- There must be 100 ways to put your eye out.

## HEADACHES

- If you eat too much sour cream, you'll get a headache.

- Wearing a hat indoors causes a headache.

- Thinking evil thoughts gives you a headache.

## STOMACHACHES

- Drink Kool-Aid straight from the package and you'll get a stomachache.

- Swallow gum and it will entangle your intestines.

- Eat raw cookie dough and you'll get a tummy ache.

- If you make yourself burp, you'll throw up.

- If you eat watermelon seeds, your stomach will burst.

- If you swallow apple seeds, a tree will grow in your stomach.

- If you don't eat your vegetables, your intestines will shut down and you'll have an awful tummy ache.

- If you eat your finger nails, they'll keep growing in your stomach until they cut through your skin.

- If you don't chew properly, you'll end up with a hole in your stomach.

## YOU'LL GET APPENDICITIS

- If you swallow grape seeds, a grape vine will grow inside and you'll get appendicitis.

- If you eat too far down the watermelon, close to the rind, you'll get appendicitis.

## AND YOU'LL GET POLIO

- If you drink milk at room temperature, you'll get polio.

- If you drink straight from the carton, you'll get polio.

- If you sit in a wet bathing suit, you'll get polio.

- If you swim in the lake, you'll get polio.

- Pull the fire alarm when there's no fire and you'll get polio.

- Run through the sprinkler and you'll get polio.

- Unless you take naps in the afternoon you'll get polio.

## YOU'LL GO INSANE

- If you keep your boots or rubbers on indoors, you'll go insane.

- Pull the curtains on nights when there's a full moon because if the rays fall on your face while you're sleeping, you'll go crazy.

• Smoke pot and you'll become a homicidal maniac.

• Aspirin with Coca-Cola will make you high and crazy.

• If you put buttons in the wrong buttonhole, you'll sew up your brain.

## YOU'LL STUNT GROWTH

• Coffee stops your growth.

• Smoking stunts your growth.

## YOU'LL GET WORMS

• You'll get worms if you eat that.

• Candy gives you worms.

• So does not washing before meals—with soap.

• Eat sugar cubes and you'll get worms in your stomach.

• Too much sugar causes worms.

• Eat raw potatoes and you'll get worms.

## WATCH YOUR FEET

• If you step on a crack, you'll break your mother's back.

• Step in a hole, you'll break your mother's sugar bowl.

- Step in a ditch, your mother's nose will itch.

- Step on the dirt, you'll tear your father's shirt.

- Step on a nail, you'll put your father in jail.

- If you don't wear Oxfords, you'll be a cripple for your whole life.

- If you wear heels, you'll break your neck.

## A BAD HAIR DAY

- If you put bobby pins into the electrical outlets, it will curl your hair.

- If you pull out a gray hair, seven will come to its funeral.

- If you set your hair with sugar water, flies will lay eggs in it.

- Combing your hair at night makes you forgetful.

- You'll get sick if you go outside with a wet head.

## POISON

- I'm closing the windows to keep out the night air; it fills the house with poison.

- Snakes poison the air with their eyes.

- The food at that Chinese restaurant is poison.

- Non-kosher food is poison.

## LET'S GO FROM THURSDAY TO SATURDAY

• Friday is the unluckiest day to be born.

• Friday is the worst day to start a new job.

• Friday is the worst day to cut your nails.

• Friday is the worst day to visit the sick.

• Friday is the worst day to start a voyage.

• Friday is the worst day to change the bed linen.

• Friday is the worst day to get sentenced for a crime.

## OTHER PHYSICAL HARM

• If you sleep with the radio on, you'll rattle your brains.

• Yawn like that and you'll get a fever.

• Flowers make the air unfit to breathe.

• Wash between your toes or mushrooms will grow.

• If you don't brush your hair, the birds will build a nest inside.

• If you wash a baby's hand, you'll wash away its luck.

• If you pop that zit, spider eggs will come out.

• If you sit on the stoop without newspapers underneath, you'll get piles.

• If you fall on your head, your kids will be born dizzy.

- If you don't brush your teeth before going to sleep, they'll fall out.

- If you don't wash behind your ears, potatoes will grow there.

- If you sit on public toilet seats, you'll get a disease.

- Don't slouch or you'll get round shoulders.

- Eating too much cereal will make you white.

- Too much TV and your brain will rot and drain out your ears.

- If you wash your face with soap and don't rinse it properly, you'll get a rash.

- If you draw one line on your hand, you'll get lead poisoning.

- If you handle a toad, you'll get warts.

- If you suck your thumb, you'll wind up with beaver teeth— and a long skinny thumb.

- If the windows aren't open at least four inches, you'll get tuberculosis . . . even in the dead of winter.

- Don't push on the soft spot on your baby brother's head; you'll squash his brains.

- If you whistle, you'll grow a beard.

- Beware of dragonflies; they sew up your mouth.

- Dragonflies sew your ears shut.

- If you read in a hammock, you'll be seasick your whole life.

- Drinking coffee will turn your neck black.

- If you ever raise a hand to hit your mother, your hand will stick up out of its grave.

- If you sniff instead of blowing your nose out, it will stay inside and glom up your innards forever.

- Flush a public john with your foot; never with your hand or you'll pick up a disease.

- Sit in a draft and you'll catch a cold.

- Don't wash a newborn's hair until he's six weeks old or he'll get pneumonia.

- You'll get black veins under your tongue if you stick it out so much.

- If you break your orthodontic braces, you'll have to wear them until you're 21.

## OTHER DIRE CONSEQUENCES

- Think something bad and God will make it happen.

- We had to cut your nails as a baby or you'd grow up to be a thief.

- If you pick dandelions, you'll wet your bed.

- If you pull your finger in church, you'll fart.

- Don't point at a grave; your finger will rot.

- Sleeping on your tummy will make you flat-chested.

- Don't enter a new house through the back door or you'll fall.

- You want triplets? Eat a tomato on your wedding day.

- She sucked her thumb so much it got all sucked away and disappeared.

- Always sleep with your head pointing north or you'll sleep poorly.

- Don't talk when you eat or a fly will zoom inside.

- If you're not in bed by eight P.M., wee Willie Winkle will come and take you away.

- Cracking your knuckles will make them bigger.

- If you swallow bubble gum, the next time you pass gas you'll blow a bubble.

- Don't dream too big or you'll be disappointed.

- Shut off the lights or you'll blow the fuses.

- Play with matches and you'll burn the house down.

- If you whistle that loud, you'll make yourself deaf.

- If you run in a storm, you'll make a path for lightning to strike.

- A dog's breath will melt your bones.

- Pepper makes your fever rise.

- Never say good-bye to someone standing on a bridge or you'll never see them again.

- Touch those red, green, or blue buttons on our Sony TV and you'll ruin the color of the picture. (They were nothing more than a logo.)

• Never open on umbrella indoors or bad things will happen.

• Stars are really angels, and if you point you might poke their eyes.

Of course, there are some terrors for which there is no solution—and a vague sense of anxiety is the order of the day.

## UNAVOIDABLE TERRORS

• The Russians are sending their troops over.

• The bogeyman will get you.

• The Japanese are going to take over the world.

• Gypsies grab little children out of cars.

• Gum takes a year to digest.

• Bite your tongue so what you've said won't come true.

# ON THE DEAD AND DYING

**When my grandfather died I was a small girl. To "protect me" the family told me he'd gone on a long trip to California. I couldn't figure out why everyone was so sad.**

- Your grandfather went with the angels to Europe to see a man about a horse.

- He's sleeping.

- He's with God.

- She's in a better place.

- She is at peace at last.

- Your puppy, Blackie, missed his mommy and daddy and that's why he was sick. So we sent him back to the puppy farm.

- I found Josh a new home.

- She would have wanted it this way.

- It didn't hurt.

- He was ready.

- She asked for you at the end.

## DEATH LORE

- When you die you go to heaven.

- This veil prevents others from catching death from me.

- We cover all the mirrors in the house when someone dies so the dead person's soul won't be caught and detained.

# Animal Fare

**Pets are as much a part of childhood as misplaced homework and muddy soccer boots. But their comings and goings—and what they do in the interval—often calls for creative cookery.**

## MAN'S BEST FRIEND (See also DEAD AND DYING)

- Your dad is allergic to dogs.

- We can't get a dog because mom is afraid of them.

- Scratch your dog where it can't scratch itself, and it will never run away from home.

- Shoopo will protect us.

- If you feed Duke your food, you'll have to eat his.

- To get that dog to stop howling, turn your shoes upside down.

- If you take your dog out when the wind is strong, he'll run around in circles.

- He likes spending the day outside (tied up/in the pen/in his cage).

- You'll get used to Rover.

- Suki's smart.

- Poopsie doesn't bite.

- Honest, it was the dog who made that smell.

- Let sleeping dogs lie or they'll bite your head off.

- If he soils the rug one more time, he's going back to the pound.

- Cats and dogs can never be friends.

- They'll fight like cats and dogs.

- She'll come home.

## THE CAT CORNER

- Cats have nine lives.

- If you torture the cat, he will dig up the flowers.

- Fluffy doesn't scratch.

- She'll love the new baby.

- Fluffy wouldn't do that!

- Cats can't fall off balconies.

- Cats know what you're thinking.

- There's more than one way to skin a cat.

- Tiger will love the new place.

## HORSE/HAMSTER (AND ASSORTED OTHER HOUSEHOLD HINDRANCES)

- He'll eat us out of house and home.

- Only rich people ride horses.

- A hamster's really a white rat.

- It's bad luck when an animal follows you home.

- I'm sure someone is desperately unhappy this stray pup is missing.

- Fish are just as interesting as a dog.

- If you handle a toad, you'll get warts.

- Birds are interesting.

- Bats are night birds.

# MENSTRUATION

**Menarche—that magic moment when a girl becomes a could-be mama—is another traditional fertile time for spin-doctoring. So is the paraphernalia associated with mother's ovulation.**

- Those [sanitary] napkins (in the bathroom) are a different kind of dinner napkin.

- They're slippers.

- I use them to clean the floor.

- No, a period is simply something that comes at the end of a sentence.

- It's a curse.

- It's a blessing.

- They call it the curse to remind us it's unladylike to use profanity.

- Eating bananas when you have your period gives you cramps.

- It's unhealthy to swim in the dog days.

- If you wash your hair during your period, it will fall out.

- If you swim during your period, you'll ruin your uterus.

- If you touch a houseplant during menstruation, it will die.

- Don't sit on cement or stone during your period or you won't be able to have babies.

- Boys don't want to go near a girl when she has her period. You're unclean then.

- It doesn't smell.

- What string? Oh, is that where I put the tea bag?

- Those cramps are all in your mind.

- You can't get your period before you're 12.

- You don't have to take gym when you have your period.

- It's a large bandage. I cut myself there.

# Clothes (Also see HAND-ME-DOWNS)

**When we were small, parents picked our wardrobes and dressed us according to their taste. Getting us to adhere to that vision as we grew often required some tall tales.**

- Boys can look up your skirt if you wear patent leather shoes.

- *Everyone's* wearing navy.

- You'll be a trendsetter.

- You don't have the legs to wear a mini.

- You're not going out like that!

- If you forget to zip your pants, a seagull will get you.

- Clean underwear prevents catastrophes.

- If your clothes are all rumpled, people will think you have no upbringing.

- Only floozies wear red boots.

- Neat clothes reflect an orderly mind.

- Your bra strap's showing: you're a tramp.

- It fits.

- They're not leg warmers; they're dancers' leggings.

- You'll grow into it.

- Girls do not wear black, except velvet-trimmed dresses.

- All eight-year-olds wear Mary Janes.

- You have a sore throat because you went out without your mittens.

- It's cold out; you'll need a coat.

# I Do

Sometimes parents had to stretch the truth a tad to present themselves in a better light to their children.

Okay, maybe we weren't the easiest kids or the most loveable. And maybe one (or both) of our parents didn't *want* to be parents, but it happened accidentally or they got pressured into it or they thought they wanted it and then were too polite or conscientious to admit the truth. The result were lies like:

- I've always wanted a family.

- My family is the most important thing in the world to me.

- I don't go out often.

- I'm not ignoring you.

- I *am* satisfied with my life.

- I have to make the calls when you come home; that's when I can reach these people.

- I am smoking to serve as a bad example to you.

- I need to run some errands.

- I never lost my temper.

- I understand.

- I never burp/belch/fart in public.

- I will never do it again.

- I believe you.

- I don't remember that.

- I just have an itch.

- I returned your phone call.

- I thought you would like it.

- I'm just tired (when really sick).

- I was just going to the store.

- I feel bad about it.

- I know what you're doing.

- I know what you're up to.

- Daddy is a zillion years old. I'm 29.

- I was a virgin when I married your dad.

- I always wanted that (a misshapen hand-made ceramic bowl).

- I never loved anyone else.

- I was popular in high school.

- I have eyes in the back of my head.

- All I care about is my family.

- If you have a different opinion I'll listen.

- I *am* listening.

# FOOD AND OTHER KITCHEN TALES

**Getting kids to try different foods required more than the patience of Job. It required the foresight and creativity of Noah.**

- What vegetables? That's a salami soufflé.

- It won't make you fat.

- Porkpie? Why it's just like cake.

- It's sauerkraut, honey. Try it. You'll like it.

- It tastes just like candy.

- You didn't touch your broccoli.

- If you eat too much candy, your teeth will fall out.

- You don't know what you're missing.

- No odor penetrates tinfoil.

- No one chews with his mouth open.

- Everyone loves fruitcake.

- No, it's not canned; it's fresh.

- I bought it from the store.

- These *are* Hostess cupcakes. It's the same thing.

- If you eat the last slice you'll be an old maid.

- That's not finger food.

- Carrots are good for your eyes.

- Brussel sprouts will make you voluptuous.

- Too much ice cream makes you burp.

- Chocolate makes you fart.

- Fish is brain food.

- Babies are starving in China because you're not eating your lamb chops.

- Liver is good for you.

- Cod liver oil is good for you.

- Cod liver oil doesn't taste bad.

- Beans don't really make you toot.

- The heel of a loaf has all the vitamins.

- Fish is the food of ghosts.

- Spinach is really cooked lettuce.

- I cooked all day for you.

- I made it the way you like it.

- I thought you'd like beets/turnips/parsnips.

- I made the cake myself.

- I love to cook.

- The store didn't have any ice cream.

- Protein is the most important food group.

- Man was meant to be carnivorous.

- Vegetarians are commie leftie hippies.

- Mussels are poisonous.

- If you swallow the seeds, a watermelon will grow in your stomach.

- Only Chinese people drink soup.

- They use Coca-Cola to clean drains; have milk instead.

- Coke and aspirin are a dangerous combination.

- Corn on the cob must be eaten with holders—and in a circular order.

- You're *supposed* to eat the cake first and save the frosting for last.

- Ice-cold food is very dangerous.

- You'll get sick if you eat traife.

- If you cut the bread from both ends, something bad will happen.

- If you leave a knife stuck in a loaf of bread, something will stick in you.

- If you toast food on a knife, you'll be poor all your life.

- Trouble befalls those who don't eat the right food.

- It should take you five minutes to clean up.

- Nobody eats their boogers.

- They're not left-overs; they're 'smores.

# MONEY

**Money has hidden meanings, bound up with our family backgrounds and feelings of security, status, and self-worth. Parents manipulate what their children know about this perhaps more than any other area save sex.**

- Money won't help.

- Money won't make you happy.

- We don't have enough money to get lunch at McDonald's.

- No one ever notices or thinks about the cost of a present.

- I didn't spend it.

- I didn't buy it because it was on sale; we needed it.

- We work hard for our money.

- I never think about money.

- If we only had money, we'd be happy.

- The one who marries for money earns it.

- If you do what you love, the money follows.

- You already get twice as much for allowance as I got when I was your age.

- *No one* gets paid to do household chores.

- We can't afford to send you to college.

- It only cost $35.

- Money is not important.

- We don't have enough money.

- We can't afford it.

- It's too expensive.

- If we wait, we can get it cheaper.

- Nobody pays retail.

- We have more than enough money.

- Money is not to be frittered away.

- We earned our money.

- We already gave at the office.

- Nobody your age gets an allowance.

- When I was your age I had to work for my money.

- That's the going rate for the Tooth Fairy.

- If you find a penny, more will follow.

- Getting an allowance will teach you about money.

- A jar of pennies in the kitchen brings good luck.

- If you save pennies, you'll never grow hungry.

- Spend like that and you'll wind up a bag lady.

- The Tooth Fairy left money under your pillow.

- If you put your money in the company pension plan, you'll never go broke.

- Stick with IBM and you'll never regret it.

- The best things in life are free.

- I worked for it; I owe it to myself.

- Money won't buy friends.

- Don't marry for money; you can borrow it cheaper.

- You can never be too thin or too rich.

- The reason we haven't bought a color TV yet has nothing to do with money; we're still waiting for them to perfect it.

- When money's found on trees, there's some grafting going on.

- It's not a sin to be rich; it's a miracle.

- When your right palm itches it means you'll come into some unexpected money; when your left one itches it means you'll have unexpected bills.

- Your dad gave me a coin to wear in my shoe at our wedding and that's why we've had a happy marriage.

- Budgeting is a fate worse than debt.

- I've got enough money to last the rest of my life.

- Money talks.

# To Explain the World/Your Disposition/ Fortunes

**Why does it thunder? What is rain? Why are you the way you are? When pressed, parents often came up with reasons. Those reasons weren't always based in fact.**

• Diamonds are the results of thunderbolts.

• Mercurochrome is monkeys' blood.

• The sky is blue.

• Thunder is the sound of God bowling.

• Thunder is God yelling.

• That crackling sound—static—is evil spirits living in your hair.

• Thunder is the sound of pins falling and lightning signals a strike.

• Rain is the angels crying.

- Rain is the angels peeing.

- Lightning is God flashing his anger.

- Lightning is God waving to get into the house.

- The moon is full of blue cheese.

- When the odometer hits 99,999, the car explodes.

- Cartoons are the same as real life.

- You're only as old as you feel.

- She's dumb because maggots ate her brain.

- Only pale, sickly people read.

- Your uncle is sick; that's why his breath smells so bad.

- We're related; this is Uncle Bob.

- Your father always has a good reason for what he does.

- You were a seven-month baby—in other words, premature.

- We did *not* put the cart before the horse.

- You're an explosive personality because you were born on a stormy night.

- You'll be rich because you were born in the afternoon.

- You have a lovely singing voice because in the hospital they rubbed an apple on your tongue.

- We knew you'd be selfish because as a baby your fists were clenched tight.

- We knew you'd be generous and kind because as a baby your fists were always open.

- We are your real parents.

## MALE/FEMALE/LOVE & MARRIAGE
## AND THEY LIVED HAPPILY EVER AFTER . . .

**Finding the right partner was hard enough. Parents putting in their two cents often made it seem impossible.**

- Ida has a fabulous son you should meet.

- Blind dates are fun.

- If you're 29 and not married, you're too fussy.

- You'll grow to love each other.

- Your mother forced me to marry her.

- You make a great couple.

- You're incomplete if you don't reproduce.

- It's just as easy to love a rich man as a poor one.

- Someday your prince will come.

- If you love someone enough, they will become worthy of it.

- Don't tell your boyfriends that you can play the piano; it will make them feel inadequate.

- You can change him.

- Men don't like to show their feelings.

- If he brings you marigolds, the relationship is going nowhere.

- The best marriages begin on a full moon—or a few days before.

- Marriage is just the first step toward a divorce.

- Your mother and I have a happy marriage.

# SCHOOL DAZE

**Getting kids to buckle down often took a gentle (or not-so-gentle) push and some keen imagination.**

- Writing (math, algebra, French, Latin, chemistry) is easy.

- Winners never quit.

- Homework is fun.

- You could have done better if you tried.

- Boys *are* better in math.

- You need to work.

- Girls *like* home ec.

- Physics is fun.

- You'll like it more in a single-sex school.

- Kids look better in uniforms.

- Your teacher asked me to give you additional practice.

- You can't graduate without knowing your multiplication tables cold.

- Geometry comes in handy later in life.

- The best part about biology is dissecting the frog.

- That should only take you half an hour to do.

- *Everyone* memorizes poetry.

- You can't graduate from third grade without knowing cursive writing.

- Shakespeare's plays are as easy to understand today as they were when they were written.

- I didn't help you *that* much with your term paper. It was really your work.

- You're going to fail science.

- Homework is good.

- Tell them you have cramps and they'll let you out of gym.

- Your teacher called.

# PROMISES UNFULFILLED

**Sometimes it seemed we were speed bumps on the super-highway of our parents' busy lives, eliciting promises from them to show up or show some interest. Often the promises fizzled away with physical separation—best friends moving, divorce. More often childhood just ran out of time.**

- I'd like to come but . . .

- We'll go on a fishing trip, just the two of us.

- We'll go bowling next week.

- I'll make it to the next hockey game.

- I'll bring the camera next time.

- I'll get there on time.

- I'll tell you later.

- I'll never hit you again.

- I'm not going to die any time soon.

- I won't get lost.

- You can pierce your ears when you're 13.

- We'll see the movie you want next time.

- She's moving away, but you'll see each other. You'll stay best friends.

- We'll go visit her next summer.

- We'll lose weight together.

- I'll get your mother to stop drinking.

- I will quit smoking.

- Your father and I will work it out.

- When I get back, things will be better between us.

- Nobody is going to jail.

- The bank won't foreclose.

- When I die I'm going to come back and haunt you.

- I'll make it up to you.

- You will never have to go and live in foster care.

- I'll drive carefully.

- I'll be back in five minutes.

# ON THE ROAD

**It's a wonder anyone traveled. If you listened to your parents, so much could go wrong on any adventure.**

• You'll have an accident.

• You'll get a speeding ticket.

• You don't know how to park.

• Never set off on a trip before a rooster crows—or you won't hear it crow again.

• You've got to pack a suit.

• You begged to go.

• It's not a nap; it's a siesta.

• It will be gorgeous this time of year.

- You can always rent a car.

- You'll get sick in Spain. Everyone does.

- You'll have a great time.

- We're almost there.

# OPTIMISM

**Not everyone's mother was Jewish. Some managed to see glimmers in even the darkest tunnels—and witticisms from the dullards. These are the optimists' daughters:**

• You're getting married in June; you don't need a back-up plan.

• You can change the world.

• It's never too late.

• I'd have to guess you'll be an artist.

• I expect great things from you.

• With that handwriting you'll probably be a doctor.

• You can be anything you want to be.

• The army is good training.

- There are lots of advantages to being a big fish in a small pond.

- That's a good school, and you can transfer later.

- You've got such extraordinary talent.

- You're going to live forever.

- You deserve it.

- Dandruff means your hair will be longer and thicker.

- Pulling out weeds is good exercise.

- If it hurts, it's not cancer.

- The world is your oyster.

- Virgo is a very good sign.

- If you never quit, you can't lose.

- You've got great genes.

- You can have it all.

- You can change.

- If you want to do something, you can find a way.

- There's nothing to be afraid of.

# FORREST GUMP LORE

**Just 'cause mama uttered it with style, doesn't mean it holds up in the real world.**

- Shoes will take you anywhere.

- Life is like a box of chocolates.

- If God had intended everyone to be the same, he'd have put braces on all our legs.

- You're no different from anyone else.

- Vacation is when you go somewhere and never come back.

- Stupid is as stupid does.

- Miracles happen every day.

- You are gifted.

- You don't know what love is.

- There's only so much fortune one man needs.

- You make your own destiny.

- You've got to put the past behind you before you can move on.

# PREJUDICE

**Our parents, no doubt, inherited their prejudices from their parents—and, in turn, tried to pass them on to their offspring with such zingers as:**

- Jewish men put you on a pedestal.

- Jews know all about money.

- Jews have horns on their heads.

- Italians make the best cooks.

- They *like* to live in one room.

- All Asians are smart.

- Asians are great violinists.

- Chinese people like to iron.

- All black people can dance.

- Hispanics multiply like rabbits.

- They're all sullen.

- All black women are strong.

- All Indians are dirty.

- Chinese people love rice.

- Women belong in the kitchen.

- Dad's job is more important.

- "Faggots" can't whistle.

- Children of older fathers are smarter.

- We're not prejudiced.

# Mom's Rules of Order

**It was mom's way or no way. And that meant no open-toed shoes after September or pierced ears before your sixteenth birthday.**

- You don't wear white shoes after Labor Day.

- You can't go to church without a hat. It's disrespectful.

- It's not ladylike to put your hands in your pockets.

- You can't be an actress. Women who are actresses are all tramps.

- *Everyone* opens presents on Christmas morning.

- *Everyone* eats Thanksgiving dinner at three in the afternoon.

- Don't change the bed linen on Friday. It isn't done.

- Children always address elders by their last names.

- It's wrong to give knives unless you tape pennies to them.

- Hear the word Hell? You must spit three times; turn around seven times, knock on wood, or touch iron.

- Everyone sends a thank-you note the day they receive a gift.

- Quality people don't wear jeans.

- You've got to pray on your knees or it doesn't count.

- It's all right to be 13 minutes late.

- Big boys don't cry.

- Only babies cry.

- Only heathens have pierced ears.

- A lady has her name in the newspaper three times: when she's born, when she marries, and when she dies.

- Little girls should always smile and be happy.

- Well-brought-up people suffer in silence.

- Women over 40 don't have long hair.

- There's a place for everything and everything has its place.

- Children aren't entitled to know.

- Children should be seen and not heard.

- Three-year-olds wipe themselves.

- Only lower-class people chew gum.

- A good woman has sex when her husband wants to.

- A good father stays home on the weekend.

- A good woman keeps a clean house.

- Good daughters call their mothers every Sunday.

- You can never have too many kisses.

- Sensible people don't want all these appliances.

- You never sit closer than 25 feet to the ocean.

- You go the bathroom every time the car stops on a long trip. (Just try and you'll make something.)

- It isn't natural, living like this.

- When you pull the larger part of the chicken breast bone, your wishes come true.

- You must always enter someplace right foot first.

- The groom carries the bride over the threshold to make sure they start married life off on the right foot.

- If you think you'll lose, you'll lose.

- Life isn't fair.

- It is better for your health to sit on the floor.

# Mom's Birth Myths

**How did you get here? To hear mom and dad tell it, there's a lot of mystery in your arrival and magic in minimizing the ordeal.**

## HOW YOU GOT HERE

- The stork brought you.

- Babies come from pumpkin patches.

- The hospital gave you to us.

- You were shipped from Cleveland.

- Babies come from your belly button.

- Storks bring babies to houses where people leave sugar cubes for them.

- You were the Immaculate Conception.

## THE PREGNANCY ITSELF AND YOUR ARRIVAL...

- I loved you from the moment I saw you.

- I was awake through the whole thing.

- Dad was in the room.

- Having you didn't hurt much.

- Having you was the most wonderful experience of my life.

- It didn't hurt when you were born because we put an ax under the bed.

- Being pregnant was the most wonderful time in my life.

- I gained 70 pounds and lost it all right away.

- We wouldn't take a boy. We told the doctor if it was a male child to leave him in the forest to starve.

- I loved breast-feeding.

- I got varicose veins from you.

- Sure your biological mother wanted you. We just wanted you more.

- You are our *real* child.

- Sure we could have children of our own, but we decided we wanted one already born.

- You never sucked your thumb.

- You were addicted to that pacifier.

- No one cares whether you breast-feed in public.

## FERTILITY RITES

- We knew you'd be a girl because we put a frying pan under the mattress.

- We knew you'd be a boy because we put a knife under the mattress.

# GOD/AFTERLIFE/THE DEVIL

**Maybe they weren't lies so much as religious lore, but could we all have been the Chosen People?**

- We are the Chosen People.

- Ours is the true religion.

- The Pope is infallible.

- God will punish you for this.

- Only good girls go to heaven.

- God likes happy children.

- Praying for something makes it happen.

- Left-handers are of the devil and you'll go to hell unless you learn to use your right hand.

- Sneezing is a breeze from Satan's wings.

- Allah created the world with a sneeze.

- You have black veins under your tongue because you stuck it out too many times at people and God is punishing you.

- Jesus Christ loves you and wants to help.

- When you stick out your tongue at your sister you are in fact sticking your tongue in the devil's butt.

- God is listening.

- Vaccinations are for people not protected by the Lord.

- God is a white man.

- God is always watching.

- We'll walk beside him in the Kingdom of Heaven.

- If you have faith, your prayers will be answered.

- Going to temple is fun.

- It's your bar mitzvah. You're a man now.

# Hi-Ho, Hi-Ho . . . It's Off to Work We Go

**The job world awaited us. And with a little parental push we knew just what direction to go.**

- Work is much more fun than fun.

- Hard work, not smart work is admirable.

- You'll be happy as a teacher.

- Advertising will be fun.

- Only you can take over the family business.

- People will respect you as a lawyer.

- You'll enjoy being a doctor.

- You'll starve as an artist.

- Write books in your spare time; you need a real job.

- It's not just nerds who are accountants.

- There's no future in acting.

- You can always fall back on your teaching degree.

# The Darker Side

**Not all lies were ego-building. Many were soul-destroying bursts of parental anger and frustration.**

- Men don't hit women.

- You're nothing.

- You'll never be anything.

- You don't deserve love.

- Boys your age act their age.

- No one will ever want you.

- You'll never amount to anything.

- It's all your fault.

- That haircut makes your face look even wider.

- You're the Devil.

- You're stupid.

- You're retarded.

- You're bad.

- The most undeveloped territory in the country is under your hat.

- You can't do anything right.

- Only the birds that sing best should sing.

- You can live without books.

- These poor grades will follow you all the days of your life.

- You're causing your grandmother to roll over in her grave.

- You're a pig.

- You're a slob.

- You're not good enough to: make the team/get into Harvard/ get invited to join the fraternity.

- You're not pretty enough to get married.

- That's too good to be true.

- Children are nature's way of telling you the party's over.

- You're spoiled.

- You were never a friend.

- You can't go home again.

- God will punish you for this.

- I shouldn't have had you.

- I wish I were dead.

- You can't.

- It's too late.

# THE ROSE-COLORED WORLD

**How to get ahead. What is the good life? Parental prescriptions for heaven on earth often revolve around strong morality and elbow grease.**

- Good things happen to good people.

- There are good people in this world and bad people in this world, and the good ones instinctively recognize each other.

- If you study hard, you'll do well in this world.

- Nobody tells family secrets.

- Good food and good habits are cheaper and better for you in the long run than bad food and bad habits.

- All drugs are bad, including coffee, tea, and Coke.

- Only hicks drink whisky, smoke cigarettes, and have tattoos.

- Good people are always kind to others.

- Good people always stick to their diet.

- Good people never yell in public.

- Nobody gets divorced.

- If you're honest and fair, things will always work out.

- You can't succeed without hard work; you can't fail with it.

- Polite people wait patiently.

# REMEDIES

**Call them old wives' tales or concoctions handed down through the ages. Sometimes they worked, sometimes they were a panacea, and sometimes they were simply a distraction to buy time and keep our minds off the problem. You decide—and perhaps you'll come away with a new remedy.**

- Warm olive oil worn under a cotton glove will fight arthritis.

- Sneeze three times and it means you're better.

- Garlic can restore your appetite.

- Tomatoes will make you want to do it (have sex).

- Oysters are an aphrodisiac.

- Wearing soiled pajamas to bed will cure bed wetting.

- If a bee buzzes, freeze and it won't sting.

- This dose of cod liver oil will fight any cold that comes along.

- Eating burnt toast clears up acne.

- Soak your face in milk every night and you'll have a youthful complexion.

- Wearing earrings improves your eyesight.

- Apply lemon juice regularly and your freckles will fade away.

- Pouring rum on your hair makes it go curly. So does squeezing grapes into your hair and eating your veggies.

- Avoid alcohol, sex, and candy and you'll live a long time.

- Soak your feet in hot mustard oil and you earrache will disappear.

- If someone pulls your ear, you'll remember your school lessons.

- Tie a string around your finger, and you'll remember your homework.

- Carry a safety pin in your purse and you'll be safe.

- An apple a day keeps the doctor away.

- Burnt toast makes teeth white.

- Throw salt on a stove to help tears dry more quickly.

# RIDICULE

**While many lies aim to reassure children, many less well-meaning ones wind up demoralizing them. Many are uttered with a heavy dose of sarcasm.**

- I didn't recognize you with that hairdo.

- You look like a gypsy.

- You're the absolute model child.

- Brilliant move.

- Way to go, Einstein.

- Let's frame this report card and send copies to all the relatives.

- Everyone else manages to find out what the homework is.

- My, don't you look nice.

• Isn't it cute the way you spelled ''meybe''?

• Oh, of course daddy loves you. We don't count love by how many presents or phone calls we get, now do we?

# REASSURANCES

**Not all lies are harmful. Often, parents tell children altruistic lies to disguise and protect—to conceal the reason for rejection and soften the blow to the child's self-respect. Sometimes they're not actually lies. Parents either see you that way or can't bear that it really isn't that way.**

• There's nothing to be afraid of.

• Those cookies you made were delicious. We ate them all.

• I love that outfit.

• You're as good as anyone else.

• You have such a beautiful face.

• You're not skinny; you're wiry.

• You're not fat; you're husky.

- Boys like something to squeeze.

- It's healthy to have a little extra meat on you.

- Twiggy was too thin; you're just right.

- Don't worry, sweetie; you'll fill out.

- It's just baby fat.

- You'll look better when your bangs are cut.

- You're perfect the way you are.

- It will look better when your hair grows in.

- No one will notice.

- On a scale of one to ten, you're a 9.5.

- It doesn't look bad.

- You *are* beautiful.

- Those glasses look great on you.

- Glasses make you look distinguished.

- You'll get taller.

- Good things come in small packages.

- You'll grow into your nose.

- Tests in junior high don't matter.

- The reason that mean guy is picking on you is because he likes you.

- I'll be here for you.

- We will always love you.

- Mommy and Daddy love each other (before a divorce).

- Trust me, no one will ever read this.

# MARTYR MOM

**Sure she fluffed flour on her face to make it look like she slaved over a hot stove and slumped onto the sofa to demonstrate how fatigued she was, but isn't that what moms do?**

• I'm doing this for your own good.

• This will hurt me more than it hurts you.

• I slaved over a hot stove because I know you like homemade spaghetti sauce.

• I left work to watch your play but now have to go back to the office until midnight.

• It's all right; I'm not hungry.

• I'd rather my children should get what they need.

• It's all right, I'll walk.

• We gave you everything.

- I was saving it for a dress for myself, but if you can't live without a Slinky, I can go without.

- I'd rather you have a violin than I get a warm coat.

- I carried you and the groceries and the stroller up five flights of stairs.

- Better you should have your teeth straightened than that I should have my leg operated on.

- It only hurts when I walk.

- Someday you'll thank me for this.

# ONE-UPMANSHIP

**Okay, so we were lazy scofflaws, ne'er-do-wells, at least when compared to our parents whose childhoods, to hear them tell it, were apparently all grueling hard work and no play. How easy we had it compared to the travails they suffered when they were our age.**

- We had to walk six miles to school every day—and back again. Often this was done:

  . . . in deep snow

  . . . barefoot

  . . . with a threadbare coat

  . . . carrying my younger brother

  . . . on an empty stomach

  . . . from an unheated home to an unheated school

  . . . uphill both ways

- We went to school on Saturdays and during the summer.

- When we were kids, the music we listened to was wonderful; not like the garbage you seem to like.

- I was never absent from school. We weren't allowed to stay home with anything less than 104-degree temperature.

- I was never late with my homework. We'd have gotten paddled for that.

- We got ten cents a week for allowance—and had to clean the house for it.

- We weren't allowed to listen to the radio until we practiced the piano for an hour.

- We each got one orange for Christmas.

- Vacation? We were too poor to go on any.

- We had to go to school year round/help out in the field/take care of the other children/work to pay for school.

- We had to share our books; we were too poor.

- I had to have a newspaper route and clerk to help out at home.

- We had no indoor plumbing. We had to use an outhouse 50/100/500 feet from the house.

- We had no animals so we were yoked to plow the field . . . barefoot.

- We had to go down to the lake to fetch fresh water.

- We didn't have enough money to take the bus.

- We remembered or they rapped our knuckles.

- Children who were disrespectful got spanked in school.

- Anything less than a B on a report card and we wouldn't be able to sit down for a week.

- We had to chop wood (to keep the TV going).

# THE WEATHER MAP

**Predicting the weather or reacting to it, parents relied on myths, legends, and conviction, administering their own brand of meteorology.**

• All children wear rubbers.

• I know someone whose eye was poked out from an umbrella.

• You can always tell a storm is coming when you see snakes dropping out of trees.

• A family song will stop the rain.

• The cat is restless because a storm is brewing.

• It never snows in the summer.

• It's too cold for shorts.

# REASSURANCES ABOUT THE FUTURE

**The sun *will* come out tomorrow—and even if rain was predicted, our parents often fortified us with visions of blue skies.**

- Your husband will take care of you.

- When you grow up you'll have a figure just like Barbie's.

- You have to learn the metric system because the whole world is going metric.

- You will grow up, get married, have children, and live happily ever after (in that order).

- If you get a good education, you'll get a good job and be financially secure.

- You'll meet somebody in college.

- You can't have a good time forever. Sooner or later you'll have to get married.

- You'll get married while you're still in college and then become a teacher.

- A summer in New Jersey will be just as much fun as a summer in Europe.

- After you marry it will all work out.

- I've got enough put aside to cover your education.

- I'll be here for you.

- We'll take care of you.

- A college degree is your ticket to success.

- Everything will be okay.

- We'll be friends for life.

- These IBM stocks will pay for your children's education.

- Real estate can only appreciate in value.

- This house will still be standing for your grandchildren.

# TALL TALES

**Every family has its "supernatural" legends that paint one of its members as a Paul Bunyan figure.**

- The dog bit me and I punched it and my arm went down its throat and I grabbed its tail and turned the critter inside out.

- Her house fell into the sea with her in it.

- Aunt Mary was a famous actress. Richard Burton asked her to marry him.

- Daddy was shot, but he was wearing his police badge and the bullet bounced off and killed the bad man who fired it.

- Uncle Harold got perfect scores on his SATs. He went to college when he was 15.

- Your grandmother is a descendant of the queen of England.

- He was the first cardinal in the United States.

- Uncle Chester won the Nobel Prize.

- Where'd I get this soda? I kicked a snowman in the ass.

- I was a fighter bomber in the Second World War. I had to parachute all over France.

- He got sucked into the toilet bowl and drowned.

- Your grandpa was able to talk to animals. They came round and helped him build this house.

- Your grandfather was shot with the archduke; that's what started the First World War.

- He led a resurrection and was shot by Hitler's troops.

- Their house was destroyed by hurricane/fire/flash/flood/tornado.

- Your grandmother walked across Europe carrying two babies.

- They took a guard hostage and broke out of Attica.

- That's a bayonet wound [appendectomy scar] from World War II.

# Rationale

**Just as parents go to great lengths to explain the mysteries of the universe and human behavior, they often justified their own actions.**

- The store was out of Cocoa Krispies.

- I don't want to hurt you.

- I'm not saying this to hurt you.

- I'm sure he was trying to reach you, but the phone was busy.

- He'll call.

- I'm doing this for your own good.

- Sending you to summer camp was for your benefit.

- Your favorite blanket fell apart in the laundry.

- I'm sorry.

# White Lies

**So many lies were polite formalities, part of the program of good manners drummed into us. Some examples:**

- I love anything made out of pipe cleaners.

- How nice to see you.

- You didn't get our postcard?

- We RSVPed.

- There's plenty to eat.

- You're looking well.

- We were just speaking of you.

- I was just going to call you.

- That's just what I wanted: the perfect gift.

- That was so kind of you.

- I'll wear it often.

- I'm going to powder my nose.

- We are so thrilled.

- Of course I remember.

# BROMIDES AND OTHER (SIGH) DECLARATIONS

**Many lies may be intentional lapses of memory, repetitions of the litanies our parents have been taught, cliches, old wives' tales, and simple misplaced convictions.**

- No, nobody called.

- It's better to be early than late.

- A bargain isn't a bargain unless you need it.

- Never look a gift horse in the mouth.

- You can never have too many kisses.

- Men will sweep you off your feet—then hand you the broom.

- Behind every great man there's a woman.

- Everything happens for a reason.

- God gives each child two parents so he or she can have a second opinion.

- You can tell the difference in tinfoils.

- Manners are your most valuable heritage.

- Bounty *is* more absorbent.

- Rock 'n' roll is just a fad.

- Your teacher knows everything.

- The gods delight in odd numbers.

- Lightning never strikes the same place twice.

- Nine is a magic number.

- That was a close one.

- The milk in back *is* fresher.

- Your thirties are your best years.

- Luck's got nothing to do with it; it's skill.

- That show is too violent.

- Scarlet eats the root and dies.

- I voted for Eisenhower.

- Great grandpa was not a horse thief.

- It isn't what you know that counts; it's what you think of in time.

- If the going seems easy, it's because you're going downhill.

- If success turns your head, you're facing the wrong way.

- Bad things happen in threes.

- It's fate.

- You don't have to do what everyone else does.

- You never call me.

- You were such a sweet child.

- Mothers are never wrong.

# Do You Behave Like Everyone Else?

From sea to shining sea, Americans are remarkably alike, incredibly different, and just plain strange. In this clever, fun and fascinating peek into the private lives of real Americans, columnist Bernice Kanner shares a delicious slice of American pie with humorous facts like:

- Of the half of us who have pets at home, 45.5% allow them in the room during sex.

- One out of every four ice cream orders is vanilla; only one in nine is for chocolate.

- Four out of ten of us admit we've been so mad we've hurled footwear at another person.

- Almost one quarter of us regularly check ourselves out in store windows and mirrors.

- 7 out of 100 Americans have flossed their teeth with their hair.

# ARE YOU NORMAL?
## BERNICE KANNER

# EMBRACE THE MISERABLE PERSON INSIDE YOU...

Your true nature is joyless and pitiful, and life is a meaningless journey of humiliation, pain and futility. With these meditations you can remind yourself, every day, of the wretched existence that is your birthright...

- I cannot retrieve my inner child, for it is dead and buried in my backyard.

- I am not afraid of failure. In fact, I'm getting used to it.

- Everyone brings something to a relationship, and to my relationships, I always bring the end.

# Meditations for Miserable People
## (Who want to stay that way)
# Dan Goodman